THE NEW CENTURY

BY PAUL RUDNICK

★

★

DRAMATISTS
PLAY SERVICE
INC.

INTRODUCTION

THE NEW CENTURY was written over a period of about ten years. PRIDE AND JOY, the opening piece, was first performed in 2005 at the Tribeca Theater Festival, where the role of Helene Nadler was played by the sublime Jackie Hoffman; Ms. Nadler was then ecstatically embodied by Linda Lavin as part of THE NEW CENTURY at Lincoln Center in 2008. Linda won a well-deserved Drama Desk Award for her work, and watching her both onstage and in rehearsal was a master class in comic technique and sheer theatrical magnetism.

PRIDE AND JOY was inspired by my meeting a batch of people with multiple gay siblings. It occurred to me that for a parent, embracing a single gay child might be a breeze, but what about, say, five gay offspring? I've also always been intrigued by the banners at gay pride events, which have been rightly expanded over the years to include not just bisexuals and the transgendered but such almost lyrical categories as the Questioning and the Two-Spirited. Helene is a bright, impressive woman navigating gale-force political correctness. The comedy in PRIDE AND JOY arises from the clash of infinite compassion and common sense.

MR. CHARLES, CURRENTLY OF PALM BEACH was first performed in 1990, at the Ensemble Studio Theater; I wrote the play for Peter Bartlett, the deliriously gifted actor who blessedly returned as Mr. Charles in THE NEW CENTURY at Lincoln Center. Christopher Ashley, who directed the play's earliest incarnations, and I once agreed that we could happily spend the rest of our lives watching Peter sip tea and chat with the audience. MR. CHARLES was written in response to the absurd notion that in order to achieve social acceptance, gay people must learn to behave themselves, and sit quietly with their hands folded. While equality, for all people, is essential, it needn't equal sameness. I'm in favor of limitless options, rather than some fresh conformity. I also believe that for any occasion, political or otherwise, Mr. Charles makes an ideal host.

CRAFTY was first performed as part of THE NEW CENTURY in 2008, where the awe-inspiring Jayne Houdyshell played Barbara

Ellen Diggs. I was first staggered by Jayne when she appeared as a neighborhood activist in Lisa Kron's glorious play WELL. Jayne somehow combines infallibly brilliant comic instincts with the most heartrending emotion; she makes both a playwright and an audience feel supremely lucky. Manhattan audiences were sometimes a bit wary of Barbara Ellen, who, as an Illinois craftsperson, was clearly from out of town, but Jayne would unfailingly win them over. I didn't write CRAFTY as a patronizing exercise; Barbara Ellen is a woman who thinks for herself, and I agree with her on just about everything. CRAFTY is about, among other things, art and survival; it's about how stitching a homemade sock monkey can be just as necessary and expressive as creating a Rembrandt or the most baroque downtown performance piece.

Sometime in 2007, I got a call from André Bishop, the Artistic Director of Lincoln Center. He'd heard about some of my one-act plays and asked if I had enough material for a full-length show. This inspired me to write the final and eponymous play of THE NEW CENTURY. I'd never thought of bringing Helene, Mr. Charles and Barbara Ellen together, and I wondered how they could ever be introduced to one another. The answer was, of course, that the only place where such disparate figures might meet would be New York City. That's one of the many reasons I love New York: It's the capital of possibility.

That's also why I love André Bishop, because he, along with Bernard Gersten, Lincoln Center's terrific Executive Producer, made THE NEW CENTURY possible. They agreed to present the plays in a splendid production at the Mitzi E. Newhouse Theater, gorgeously directed by Nicholas Martin, who provided an atmosphere of joy and acceptance.

THE NEW CENTURY was a deeply happy experience for me, and not just because — since my plays were being done at Lincoln Center — there were NEW CENTURY baseball caps, mugs and refrigerator magnets. THE NEW CENTURY was one of those moments where, particularly thanks to Mr. Bishop, everything went right. The cast, which also included the sly and delightful Mike Doyle as both David Nadler and Shane, and the giddy and skillful Christy Pusz as Joanne, was ideal; the design team was impeccable, the stage management, backstage crew and understudies were a dream, and I became utterly and gratefully spoiled.

On a certain level, THE NEW CENTURY is a party, where the most unlikely people get to meet and surprise themselves. They also get to move cautiously yet optimistically forward, and they find that a little dancing never hurts.

—*Paul Rudnick*

THE NEW CENTURY was produced by Lincoln Center Theater at the Mitzi E. Newhouse Theater (Bernard Gersten, Executive Producer; André Bishop, Artistic Director) in New York City, opening on April 14, 2008. It was directed by Nicholas Martin; the set design was by Allen Moyer, the lighting design was by Kenneth Posner; the costume design was by William Ivey Long, the original music and sound design were by Mark Bennett; the general manager was Adam Siegel, the stage manager was Stephen M. Kaus; and the production manager was Jeff Hamlin. The cast was as follows:

HELENE NADLER .... Linda Lavin
DAVID NADLER/SHANE .... Mike Doyle
ANNOUNCER .... Jordan Dean
MR. CHARLES .... Peter Bartlett
JOANN MILDERRY .... Christy Pusz
BARBARA ELLEN DIGGS .... Jayne Houdyshell

TABLE OF CONTENTS

PRIDE AND JOY

PLACE

A high school or community college conference room or small auditorium on Long Island. A sign or banner hangs on a wall or curtain; the banner has the initials: P.L.G.B.T.Q.C.C.C. & O.

TIME

Early evening, a weeknight.

PRIDE AND JOY

Lights up on Helene Nadler, an attractive Long Island matron, seated on a folding chair. Helene is smartly dressed and accessorized; she's a proud, intelligent, well-spoken woman. She can be gracious, charming and, when necessary, enraged. She speaks to the audience.

HELENE. Good evening. Hi. My name is Helene Nadler, and if I seem a little nervous, it's because this is my very first time here at a meeting of the Massapequa chapter of the Parents of Lesbians, Gays, Bisexuals, the Transgendered, the Questioning, the Curious, the Creatively Concerned and Others. Of Color. With Colds. No, I'm sorry, I'm kidding, maybe we should just call this group, "Why Jimmy Has No Friends." I'm kidding! Because we are all proud, because we are all special. And I am here to tell you, to prove to you, that I am the most accepting, the most tolerant, and the most loving mother *of all time.* Bar none. *You hear me?*

Oh, I know what you're thinking, each and every one of you, you're thinking your child was different, your little bubble went through tough times, your little sweetheart was a total nightmare and you were still warm and nonjudgmental and loving and hugging and giving them self-esteem — well, fuck you. You are nothing. And you will bow down! *(Pulling herself together.)*

I'm sorry. It's just, well, you'll see. What I've been through. It all started ten years ago, with my eldest child, my daughter, Leslie. "Leslie" — what was I thinking? She was twenty-two, she said, "Mother" — so I knew it wasn't happy talk, "Mother, I have something to tell you. I'm a lesbian." And I took a deep breath and I said, Leslie — look at yourself. You're a professional tennis player, you have two cats, named Alice and Mrs. Dalloway, you live with a female social worker and you have the same haircut as a twelve-year-old Amish boy. Of course you're a lesbian. I've been telling you that for years. Helen Keller would know you were a lesbian, from the stubble. And she was so happy, she said, so you don't hate me? And I said, of course I hate you, but not because you're a lesbian.

I hate you because you're so boring. Why can't you be like Melissa Etheridge or Ellen Degeneres, okay, it's always pants, but at least they're Prada. They're cute! They're fun! And we're both thrilled, because it's all out in the open, we're free, we're clean, well, not their apartment. I said, girls, what is that aroma, kitty litter and patchouli? Is that some new Glade spray, Country Fresh Lesbian? Jodie Foster Number Five? But I don't care, I still visit, I sit on their couch, because I am the most loving mother of all time! Wait.

One year later, my middle child, my son, Ronnie, he comes to me. "Ronnie" — do I learn? And he says, Mom, I have something to tell you. And I say, you're gay, it's swell, no problem, *Angels*, Elton John, *Will and Grace* — I loved that show, it was adorable, it was like if Pottery Barn sold people. But Ronnie says, no, it's not that. He says, I was born into the wrong body. And I say, so was I, it's called Atkins, get over it. And he, no, I was born into the wrong gender. I was meant to be a woman. And I have to sit down. I mean, Ronnie is six three with a beer gut and hairline problems, and all I'm thinking is, Ronnie, which woman? Ed Asner? And he says, Mom, can you imagine what it's like, always feeling so uncomfortable, so totally out of place, he says, Mom, think how you felt when we had to spend Passover with Daddy's family, in New Jersey, and I say, Ronnie, chop it off! If you want a vagina, here's the Visa!

So a year later, I'm riding high, I'm thinking, look at my beautiful family, there's Leslie and Marsha, that's her partner, they announced it in the *Times*, did you see the photo? "Dennis the Menace Marries Opie." And they're having a baby. They wanted to make sure it was multicultural, so at the sperm bank they requested Vietnamese, Jamaican or Nigerian, I said, great, they can just attach the sperm to the menus and slide it under the door. But I'm thrilled for them, and in comes Ronnie, excuse me, Veronica, in her pale yellow ruffles and her pearls, and I just think — she's lovely. And I'm so proud of her. And where do you find a wrap skirt in that size? And then she says, and Mom, I want you to meet someone, my girlfriend, Renee. And in walks this pretty little thing, she's a flight attendant on United, and I say, excuse me, and Veronica says, and I'm also a lesbian. And I pause and I say, Ronnie, didn't you take the long way around? And she, see, I said she, she says, no, when I was a man, I could never enjoy sex with a woman, but now that I'm a woman, I think it's the most beautiful experience ever. And I'm thinking, Jesus Christ, for what we spent on hormones, I could've had a new kitchen. And Marsha starts eyeballing Renee and Veronica's getting all huffy, and Leslie's got morning sickness, and I'm about to jump out the window but I go to the powder room, I splash some water on my temples and I say, Helene — you can do this. You are the most incredible, loving mother on earth, you can go for the gold, for the platinum, and I burst back into the room and I say, you are all so wonderful and so special, and the front door opens, and it's my baby, my David, and he says, Mom, I have something to tell you.

And I'm giddy, I'm flying, I say, so what could it be, you're gay, you're transsexual, you're a pregnant Nigerian lesbian flight attendant — the woman they could never fire. Whatever you are, I love you. And he says, okay, first off, I'm gay. And I say, yawn. Next. And he says, I am also — seriously into leather. And I say, great, I'm into fur. And he says, no, I'm the President of the International Order of Gay Leathermen, which is dedicated to the practice of bondage, sado-masochism, verbal abuse and scatology. And Veronica looks at Leslie, who rolls her eyes and says, "Yale."

And David says, my personal favorite is scatology. *(To the audience.)* This is the clincher. This is my Purple Heart, my Nobel Prize in motherhood! He says that scatology involves enemas. People peeing on each other. And worse. Use your imagination. No, don't. And I look at him, and for a second I lose it, I become so intolerant, I become my mother, and I say, David, in this house we use the toilet, not a friend from Tribeca! And David says, it's all completely safe and careful, it's about the erotic aspects of defecation, he says that children play happily with their own feces until society tells them to be ashamed, and I say, not Jewish children! You never had to play with shit, we gave you Mattel! And he says, Mom, I love you so much, and I just want to share my life openly. And I'm about to say, please don't share anything that leaves a stain. And Leslie touches my hand, and I stop. And I think, so many people's children, they hide everything. They live separate, secret lives. They're like strangers. *I love those children.*

And that night, after everyone leaves, I turned to my husband and I said, Morris, I gave birth to three perfect children — *what did you do to them?* And he said, they're still perfect, and I said, sure, if we're making a documentary. What should we call it — *Guess What's Coming to Dinner*? *Hide Your Pets*? And he said, don't drive yourself crazy, and I said, but they're our children, doesn't it bother you? And he says, not one bit, and I ask, but why not? And he says, because whenever they come over, I just turn off my hearing aid. And I said, oh my God, and he asks, but who's that big girl, the one who looks like Ronnie?

And he said, come to bed, but I couldn't sleep, and then it's three A.M. and I fell to my knees and I cry out to God! I say, why me? I go to temple, I pay my taxes, our housekeeper has health insurance, and probably my best diamond earrings! And then I felt ashamed, I felt hopelessly conventional, but goddamnit, I still wanted an answer! And then, just as I was finishing my third all-butter French crumbcake, I had — a vision. Sugar shock, maybe, carb coma, fine — but there she was! An Asian woman, a Chinese, in the little black outfit, standing right near my breakfront. And she said, I am the mother of Chang and Eng, the famous Siamese twins.

And the mother, she says, when my boys were born, I also cried out. I said, why are my children so different, so odd, so — hard to shop for? And I wanted to comfort her, can you imagine, Siamese twins? All I kept thinking about was — long car trips. And the twins are in the backseat and they're fighting, he touched me, he called me a name — and you can't separate them. But the mother, she said, when my babies were born, I looked at them wriggling in their cradle, like paper dolls made of flesh, and through my heartache, a thought arose — at least, they will never be alone. And I thought to myself, I thought, all of my children, with all of their mishegas, maybe all they're doing is finding very individual, very new, and very irritating ways — not to be lonely.

And the next morning, not only did I feel so much better, but I realized, not only was I a proud and loving Mom, but — I could compete! That erotic poop thing pushed me right over the top! So here now, I would like you to meet my pride and joy, my Academy Award for Best Mother Ever …

(She points to someone in the audience.) I'm talking to you, Marilyn Schwartz, with your little bisexual corporate attorney son — big fuckin' deal! May I present *my* son, Dr. David Benjamin Nadler! *(David Nadler enters, dressed head to toe in aggressive black leather, including a motorcycle jacket, a harness and chaps. His head and face are completely obscured by a full leather hood. He waves to*

the audience.) Isn't he gorgeous? Well, take my word. Look at him, he's heaven … *(She's stroking his leather jacket.)* He's like a Coach bag. And you know, in many ways, he's the perfect son. He's a doctor, and he's a slave. *(David nods in agreement.)* David — clean your room. *(She unzips the zipper which covers David's mouth.)*
DAVID. Yes, master.
HELENE. Mother.
DAVID. Yes, Mother.
HELENE. *(To the audience.)* Could you die? *(To David.)* Kiss your Aunt Sylvia.
DAVID. *(Whining.)* Do I have to?
HELENE. *(Grabbing his dog collar.)* What was that, slave?
DAVID. *(Obeying instantly.)* Yes, Mother. *(Helene laughs, delighted with her power.)*
HELENE. *(To the audience.)* You can make him do anything except heavy lifting. He has a bad back. I don't know how Jewish men ever built the pyramids.
DAVID. Mother!
HELENE. *(To David, very commanding.)* Come for the weekend, and *stay over.*
DAVID. But I have stuff to do! *(Helene hurls David to the ground, and stands over him.)*
HELENE. What was that, slave?
DAVID. Mother, I'm very busy!
HELENE. Too busy for your own family?
DAVID. I have my own life!
HELENE. What was that, pussy boy?
DAVID. Yes, Mother.
HELENE. I love it! I love all my children! I win!
DAVID. I have to go. *(David exits.)*
HELENE. On the paper! *(To the audience.)* Thank you! Good night! *(The lights dim, as Helene bows and then follows her son offstage. Curtain.)*

End of Play

MR. CHARLES, CURRENTLY OF PALM BEACH

PLACE

A bare-bones public access television studio in Florida.

TIME

Early evening.

MR. CHARLES, CURRENTLY OF PALM BEACH

A video camera is mounted on a tripod and aimed at a platform which supports the flamboyant, if limited, set for Mr. Charles' cable show. There is a suitably fussy folding screen, a small, ornate French writing desk, holding a silver tea service and an artificial floral arrangement, and a gilded, throne-like French chair set center stage. There is a small table beside the chair.

ANNOUNCER.   And now ladies and gentlemen, direct from Palm Beach, cable channel 47 is proud to present, the gayest man in the universe — it's Mr. Charles! *(Buoyant, big band theme music is heard, something very upbeat and welcoming. Mr. Charles enters. He is ageless; he is stylish, haughty and bold. He wears a fairly obvious, fairly blonde hairpiece, a tomato red blazer over a gingham shirt, with an Hermes scarf knotted apache-style at his throat, colorful espadrilles, white, lemon, or lime green slacks, and a necktie knotted as a belt. His face boasts a not particularly discreet coat of moisturizer, bronzer and a touch of mascara. His image is not transvestite but Palm Beach decorator or antiques dealer. He is glorious. After smiling and posing for the audience, Mr. Charles picks up a letter from the small table.)*
MR. CHARLES. *(Reading from the letter.)* "What causes homosexuality?" *(He puts the letter down.)* I do. I am so deeply homosexual, that with just a glance, I can actually turn someone gay. *(He glances at someone in the audience.)* Well, that was easy. Sometimes, for a lark, I like to stroll through maternity wards, to upset new parents. I am Mr. Charles, and I am currently residing here in Palm Beach, in semi-retirement. In exile. You see, I was asked to leave New York. There was a vote. Today's modern homosexuals find me an

embarrassment. This is because, on certain occasions, I take what I call — a nelly break. For example: A few months ago, I attended an NYU conference, on gay role models. And this young man stood up and said … *(In an earnest and manly voice.)* "We must show the world that gay people are not just a pack of screaming queens, with eye makeup, effeminate hand gestures and high-pitched voices." And I just said … *(He stands and does a nelly break, shrieking and mincing and flapping his wrists; he might burble, "Oh girl! Oh Miss Thing! Oh Mary!" Then he stops and sits, instantly calm again.)* It just happened. I went nelly. I just began babbling, in Gay English. You know, Shebonics. Oh, or another time, I was attending a rally. And a woman approached me and she said, "I would like you to donate five thousand dollars, to support our boycott of Hollywood films which portray homosexuals as socially irresponsible, promiscuous, and campy." *(Another delirious nelly break.)* And so, I was asked to leave the city. As revenge, I have begun to broadcast this program on cable channel 47, a show which I call "Too Gay." It can be found at four A.M. on alternate Thursdays, in between "Adult Interludes" and "Stretching with Sylvia." Poor dear. I would now like to introduce a very popular feature of this program, my devoted companion, Shane. *(Shane, a dim, affable, low-rent hunk enters, wearing a tight tank top, warm-up pants and sneakers, Shane eyes the audience and the camera. Shane and Mr. Charles get along just great; they appreciate each other.)*

SHANE. *(To the audience.)* Hey.

MR. CHARLES. Shane is my ward. I first met him three weeks ago, at a fabulous local night spot, the Back Alley. Shane was appearing atop a plywood cube. He is a gifted performer. *(Mr. Charles motions to an offstage sound booth and hot dance music blares. Shane's head jerks up, and he begins to dance, pinching his own nipples and then exploding into a demented frenzy. Mr. Charles motions for the music to stop, and Shane stops dancing.)* Thank you, Shane.

SHANE. You got it. *(Shane exits.)*

MR. CHARLES. He lives to dance. Since I have begun these broadcasts, I have received many letters and postcards, including this telegram, from the National Gay Task Force in Washington. *(He picks up a telegram from the table.)* It reads … *(Reading the telegram.)* "Dear Mr. Charles. Stop." *(He puts down the telegram.)* I would now like to answer several of the many queries I have received regarding homosexuality. Shane? *(Shane enters, now wearing a homemade Robin costume, which includes tight green trunks, a yellow satin cape worn over a tight red tank top, and a black mask. He is not happy about this outfit. He carries a stack of letters, which he dumps on the table. Then he poses, with his hands on his hips, as a superhero.)*

SHANE. Man, I don't know about this outfit.

MR. CHARLES. It doesn't bother Robin.

SHANE. I ain't Robin.

MR. CHARLES. Oh, but you could be.

SHANE. Yeah? Do you think that Batman and Robin, like, do it?

MR. CHARLES. Do you?

SHANE. Yeah, I bet that like, after they nail some robbers and save Gotham City, they're like, all fired up, so they, like, do some X and stay out all night.

MR. CHARLES. Indeed. And we could dress up and go in their place. Only we would fight — bad taste. We would burst into peoples' homes and proclaim, "We have come to save you! From that terrible armoire!"

SHANE. Yeah! *(Shane exits.)*

MR. CHARLES. He hides his pain. *(He picks up a letter.)* "Dear Mr. Charles, Nowadays, is there any difference between a gay man and a straight man?" None whatsoever. They are identical. In fact, you may be sitting next to a gay man at the theatre and not even know it. But here's a clue: He's saving his Playbill. And he's awake. *(Another letter.)* "Dear Mr. Charles, Can gay people change?" Of course — for dinner. *(Another letter.)* "Should gays be allowed to serve in the military?" Absolutely! You see, I have this military fantasy. Shane? *(Shane enters, now wearing fatigue shorts, an olive green military tank top, and a military cap. Shane holds a video camera on his shoulder and follows Mr. Charles during the next segment, acting as Mr. Charles' personal cameraman. Mr. Charles stands, and acts out his fantasy.)* I'm serving in Vietnam, with my unit. And one night, I traipse into the shower tent. It's after hours, and I'm just wearing my kimono, mules and a light moisture pack. And I hear the sound of rushing water … *(Shane discreetly makes the sound of rushing water.)* And I turn, and there at the end of a row of showers stands a naked marine. John McCain. His flesh glistens as he lathers up, he runs the soap over his firm chest, his washboard stomach, down, down, into his manly areas. My breathing grows heavy as my kimono falls from at least one shoulder, and I stand beneath the showerhead beside him, attaching my plastic shower caddy, which contains my shampoo, conditioner, finishing rinse and scented bath gelee. My eyes are everywhere, feasting on his shining, sudsy, gleaming male flesh. Finally, I speak. "Hello, soldier," I murmur. "Loofah?" We could transform the armed forces. Make remarks, not war. Thank you, Shane. As you were. *(Shane salutes and exits, as military music plays. Picking up another letter:)* "Should gays be allowed to marry?" Of course, wealthy, older women. *(Another letter.)* "Can you always tell if someone is gay?" Well, I can. There's always a giveaway, sometimes it's just a glance on a street corner, or a slight moan during oral sex. But I do have a question. When an English person comes out, is anyone really surprised? Did anyone say, "Oh no, not *Ian McKellan?" (Another letter.)* "Dear Mr. Charles, I am a lesbian." Doesn't that sound like some marvelous first line from Dickens? "I am a lesbian. All you do on your show is talk about gay men. What about gay women?" *(He stands and smiles, very graciously.)* Lesbians. I could write a cookbook. But let us not resort to easy stereotypes, picturing all gay women as husky, can-do gals, out hiking in their flannel and sensible shoes. A gay woman is not simply Paul Bunyan with a cat. *(By this point Mr. Charles has poured himself a cup of tea from the silver tea service. He notices that Shane has neglected to provide a lemon wedge on the tray. He calls out, sharply.)* Shane? Shane! *(Shane hurries in, holding out the lemon wedge, which he squeezes into Mr. Charles' cup of tea, and exits, as cheery music plays.)* Danke, Shane. *(He sips his tea.)* Lesbians are charming, endlessly varied people, with all sorts of haircuts, from the flattop to the pixie. I, in fact, have taken a lesbian into my home. *(He holds a finger to his lips — shh!)* She's asleep in the basement until Spring. *(Another letter.)* "How can I raise gay-positive children in today's political climate?" Well, there are many politically aware children's books, including *Daddy's Roommate* and *Heather Has Two Mommies*. I will soon be publishing my additions to this series. My children's books will include *Uncle Patrick Has a Beautiful Apartment* and *Aunt Cathy's Large Friend. (Another letter.)* Oh look, here's a letter for Shane. *(He sniffs the letter, which is perfumed.)* Oh, Shane! *(Shane enters.)*

SHANE. Yeah?

MR. CHARLES. *(Pointing to the words as he reads.)* "Dear Shane." *(Shane grins and grunts, very pleased.)* "I think that you are the hottest thing in South Florida. I loved you on last week's show, when you were dressed as Tarzan." *(The Tarzan outfit was Mr. Charles' idea, and*

Shane grimaces at the memory.) You see? "But why don't you dump Mr. Charles and get your own show?"

SHANE. *(Pleased.)* It says that?

MR. CHARLES. Well, Shane, do you think you're ready?

SHANE. Well, you know, I've been thinkin' about it. I could do like a game show and I would ask people questions about like *Star Wars* and other game shows. And I would call it, *Are You Smarter Than Shane?*

MR. CHARLES. *(Encouragingly.)* That's good.

SHANE. Or I could help people, I could like go around the country and find poor people and these like amazing families living in shacks with like twenty-eight handicapped kids, and I could teach 'em to dance!

MR. CHARLES. *(Thrilled.)* I can see it!

SHANE. And ya know what I would call it, that show, to like inspire people?

MR. CHARLES. Yes?

SHANE. *The Shane Show.*

MR. CHARLES. By all means!

SHANE. *(Into the camera.)* Watch for it! *(Shane executes a demented martial arts/karate move, with a cry of "Hyah!" and exits.)*

MR. CHARLES. They grow up so fast. *(Another letter.)* "Dear Mr. Charles, Do you enjoy gay theater?" I am gay theater. Alright, I will now give you the entire history of American gay theater, in sixty seconds. Go! *(Mr. Charles stands, and there's a dramatic lighting change, as he free-associates rapidly, using various voices and accents.)* "Jimmy isn't like the other boys — do you know what you are — he's no son of mine! I'm just so lonely and sick of my own evil — he was a boy, just a boy — Skipper was my buddy, and our love was pure and strong, but those things they're saying, they're true about me! I'm so sick and ashamed, Karen! Do you know what you are? I am a thirty-two-year-old pockmarked Jew fairy, and that was when my father saw me backstage, in my wig and my tights, and he said, take care of my son. *(Singing.)* I am what I am! *(In a gravelly, Harvey Fierstein voice.)* I just wanna be loved, is that so wrong? But Doctor, what's wrong with David, with all the Davids? Our people are dying, and the Mayor still won't even say the name of the disease — Maria Callas! *(He raises his arms, as graceful wings.)* Let the great work begin! *(He raises his arms again.)* Let the great work begin, part two! When you speak of gay theater, and you will

— be kind. Because it's all about love, valour, baseball, and gratu-
itous frontal male nudity! *(Shane enters, naked, and hands Mr.
Charles a bouquet of roses, as triumphant Oscar Night music soars.)*
Bravo! *(Mr. Charles bows deeply as Shane exits.)* Which brings us to
my favorite part of the program, a forum which I call, "People I
Hate." This week's person I hate most in the world is someone I've
never even met. His name is Theodore DiBenedetto, and he wrote
this letter to the editor of our local paper. *(Mr. Charles reads aloud
from a copy of the newspaper, using a butch, manly voice.)* "Dear *Palm
Beach Sentinal*, I am a gay man who owns the East Bay Hardware
Store." *(He looks up with a withering glance and then continues.)*
"And I am sick and tired of gay people demanding equal rights
when they keep behaving like freaks. As gay people, we must prove
that we aren't just stereotypes. We must demonstrate that our lives
are normal and wholesome. We must show that we can hold jobs,
go to church and raise children, just like anyone else. This is how
we will earn our place at the table." *(Mr. Charles puts down the
paper. He is now dangerously angry, like steel.)* Darling, I *set* the table.
I arranged the flowers. And I would rather have Shane's knife at my
throat then share even a brunch with Mr. DiBenedetto and his
kind. The nice boys. The good citizens. But please, Mr.
DiBenedetto, if you'd like, by all means, be normal and wholesome
and responsible, get married, have children, move to the suburbs.
I'll wait here. Oh, and Mr. DiBenedetto, by the by … *(Mr. Charles
stands and launches into a viciously savage nelly break, directly into the
camera. He becomes a ferocious nelly whirlwind, making enormous
flamboyant gestures to the audience. He might look into the camera
and elaborately mime applying lipstick, and licking his forefinger and
slicking each eyebrow. Finally he turns, rump to the camera, and
minces back to the chair, his heels off the ground, as if he were wearing imaginary spike heels. He turns, sits, and arranges his wrists. With
a knife-edge flourish, he crosses his legs. Shane enters, wearing white
jeans and an untucked Versace shirt.)*
SHANE. Um, I gotta go out, okay?
MR. CHARLES. Do you have to get your hair cut?
SHANE. Yeah, um, right!
MR. CHARLES. Did you take the car keys?
SHANE. *(Holding up the keys.)* Right here!
MR. CHARLES. *(Like a doting parent.)* And all of the cash on my
dresser, my credit cards, and my mother's emerald earrings from

my sock drawer?

SHANE. Got 'em!

MR. CHARLES. Do you love me forever?

SHANE. Yeah, of course!

MR. CHARLES. *(Delighted.)* On your way!

SHANE. Later! *(Shane exits.)*

MR. CHARLES. Oh, he's not fooling me. He doesn't need a haircut. Ah, but I am the last of my kind. I shall perish, like the dinosaur. Unless, of course, Steven Spielberg discovers some ancient DNA from Paul Lynde and makes more. But let me ask you something, all of you. Have you ever been in love? Hands? You see, I fell in love quite early. I must have been, oh, twelve? I had just been savagely beaten by … *(He tries to remember, quite cheerfully.)* oh, it could have been anyone. But this was at school. I came home bruised, caked with mud. I ran up to my room, and I looked in the mirror. And I thought, all right, whom would I rather be? The boys who beat me up, the boys who played baseball and caught frogs and were already losing their figures? Or would I rather be — Mr. Charles. Who even at twelve knew how to turn his face so the tears would glisten. Who knew enough to immediately put Billie Holiday on the hifi, and lip-synch. Who could transform a schoolyard humiliation into an Academy Award. And that was when I fell passionately in love — with being gay. Oh, there have been men, and boys, and Wedgewood. But being gay — there's a romance. *(Shane enters.)*

SHANE. Hey, Chuck?

MR. CHARLES. You're back.

SHANE. When I was drivin' to the club, I was thinkin' about like, what you said at the beginning of the show, that you can, like, make people gay, just by lookin' at 'em?

MR. CHARLES. In my time.

SHANE. Well, I was kinda wonderin', I mean, nowadays, most gay guys just wanna be, like, regular people. And the world's already got lots of them. So what I was thinkin' was, could you make some more of you?

MR. CHARLES. Oh no, I don't think so, nobody wants to be truly gay anymore. It's passé.

SHANE. So, like, kick their ass! You could do it. Use your superpowers. Your gay ray. Make an army. A planet!

MR. CHARLES. It's tempting …

25

SHANE. Go for it, man!

MR. CHARLES. You're too sweet.

SHANE. Later! *(Shane exits.)*

MR. CHARLES. Well, let me see, how would I do this? Make more? *(He looks at the audience.)* Yes — the receptionist. With the baby. Could you come down here? *(Joann Milderry, the studio receptionist comes onstage, carrying her seven-month-old baby. Joann is sweet, very young, shy and apologetic.)*

JOANN. *(Timidly, hovering.)* Really?

MR. CHARLES. Yes, it's fine, please, come on down.

JOANN. I'm so sorry, but my boyfriend sort of — disappeared, and my Mom usually watches the baby but she was mad at me. She thinks that I shouldn't be working here. She thinks you're too weird.

MR. CHARLES. But why?

JOANN. *(Cautiously pointing to his hairpiece.)* I think it's your hat.

MR. CHARLES. Aha.

JOANN. But I told her that I like it here — I like you.

MR. CHARLES. Stop.

JOANN. *(Joann starting to exit.)* Okay.

MR. CHARLES. Figure of speech. And what a beautiful child. Boy or girl?

JOANN. A boy. Max.

MR. CHARLES. *(To the baby.)* How would you like to grow up like me? How would you like to be — Mr. Max?

JOANN. Could you really make him — like you?

MR. CHARLES. Is there a problem?

JOANN. Well — would he have a difficult life?

MR. CHARLES. Who doesn't?

JOANN. Will people be mean to him?

MR. CHARLES. *(Cheerfully.)* Of course.

JOANN. Will he do those — nelly breaks?

MR. CHARLES. Sometimes — in front of your mother. Think how upset she'll be.

JOANN. *(Firmly holding out the baby.)* Do it.

MR. CHARLES. Are you sure? It's a big step.

JOANN. Well — did you ever see that movie, *The Wizard of Oz*?

MR. CHARLES. Look at me.

JOANN. You know how that main girl, what's her name?

MR. CHARLES. Dorothy?

JOANN. Right, Dorothy, well, at the beginning of the movie, she's back home on the farm in Kansas, and the movie's in black and white. But then, when she gets to Oz, everything's in color. So it's like, my life, and my baby's life, at least right now, we're in Kansas. But someone like you, and I don't know if it's because you're gay or what, but — you're in color.

MR. CHARLES. Then here we go! *(Mr. Charles aims two fingers at the baby and makes a small hissing noise, zapping the baby.)* Ssst! He's on his way!

JOANN. To Oz, or New York or, I don't know, to wherever you buy your clothes?

MR. CHARLES. Who knows?

JOANN. Thank you. *(As she exits, to the baby.)* He's a very nice man.

MR. CHARLES. *(To the departing mother and child.)* Have fun! He will! *(Joann and the baby exit. Mr. Charles speaks to the audience.)* Oh, I know what you're thinking. You're thinking, oh please, he doesn't really have any powers. He's just another shrill, aging Palm Beach queen with too many cocktails and a bad hairpiece. Well, would you like to hear something even more horrible, my pretties? It isn't a hairpiece. *(Mr. Charles cackles gleefully and gestures grandly to his hair.)* It's MINE! *(As the peppy theme music from his show is heard he makes a little pouting face, then he begins blowing kisses and waving goodbye, as the lights fade. Curtain.)*

End of Play

CRAFTY

CRAFTY

Barbara Ellen Diggs stands in a conference room of a municipal building in Decatur, Illinois. Barbara Ellen is a sweet-faced, extremely good-natured, outgoing woman, wearing a sweatshirt with a floral appliqué or a hand knit sweater. She is surrounded by tables holding many homemade craft items.

BARBARA ELLEN. Hi. I'm Barbara Ellen Diggs, and I'm a craftsperson here in Decatur. And this morning I would like to speak to you, our Junior Chamber of Commerce, on the critical importance of crafts in our culture. Before I discovered crafts, I suffered from clinical depression and had no self-esteem; but today I exhibit my work statewide and I teach workshops at our local women's prison, where a lady who slaughtered her entire family now makes notecards personalized with sequins and dried corn. I have invented over five hundred and twelve different saleables for Christmas bazaars, including doorknob covers, *(She holds up a board holding three doorknobs with crocheted holiday covers.)* microwave bonnets *(She holds up a large quilted microwave bonnet.)* and toilet paper caddies *(She holds up a crocheted cover for a roll of toilet paper.)* And I have recently hand-crocheted a tuxedo for my toaster. *(She holds up a toaster dressed in a hand crocheted black and white cover with a bowtie.)* For wardrobe items I practice appliqué, which is the art of heat-bonding a felt Santa or a three-dimensional chenille snowman onto a garment. *(She holds up a sweatshirt appliquéd with a snowman and a Santa.)* Last Christmas, across a particularly memorable sweatshirt, I created an entire colonial village, including an ice-skating pond, a blacksmith's shop, and a mischievous Jewish peddler. I also deeply enjoy scrapbooking. *(She picks up a scrapbook and opens it to a page, showing it to the audience as she points to various features.)* For example, on this page, I color-xeroxed a simple Polaroid of my Aunt Polly, and I placed the image at the center of a piece of oaktag. Then I surrounded the picture with heart-shaped lace doilies, crepe-paper rosettes, and silk ribbon worked to spell out "Aunt Polly." I've also included some ticket stubs from a movie we saw together, *That Darn Cat*, the invitation to her wedding to Uncle Walt, and a tiny burlap bag containing one of her kidney stones. The page now weighs over fifteen pounds, and it can tell you Aunt Polly's entire life story, and I don't even like her.

I am currently applying for a grant for what I consider to be a truly American crafts milestone: I intend to create a series of commemorative plaques, saluting the history of American crafts. Each plaque will be devoted to celebrating a separate medium of expression, including buttons, decals, colored gravel, bottle-caps, pop-tops, tissue paper, construction paper, mosaic tile, hooked rug, rag rug, needlepoint, needlepoint-in-a-tube, wood-burning, copper tooling, coffee cans, lanyards, embossing, vinyl, leather, leatherette, nauga, look-of-nauga, Dixie cups, styrofoam, balsa wood, spray snow stenciling, corkware, potholder loops, macaroni collage on Michelob beer bottles, popsicle sticks, cheese sculpture, scented soap, scented beeswax, acrylic modeling clay, and human hair. My primary expenses will be for labor, Zoloft, and glue.

Some sophisticated people say that crafts aren't art, but by the same token, some people say that New Yorkers aren't people. Crafts allow me to express myself, to create something worth dusting. When I pick up a crochet hook or a staple gun I'm tingling. I'm transported. This one time I started rubber cementing sea shells onto a keepsake box as a baby gift, and by the time I looked up, that child was in college.

My family has always been very supportive of my hobbies, well, except for my son, whom I loved dearly. Hank was always — very special. He always used to scold me for using words like that, what did he call them — euphemisms. He said, Mom, I'm gay. And I said, no you're not, you're special. And he said no, that makes me sound like I'm retarded. And I would say, I wish. And we would laugh. It never really bothered me, even though he did move away and started working for a fancy Broadway costume designer in New York and he didn't come back home all that often. But we would write back and forth, and he would send me trims and braid, all these beautiful expensive things from the costumes and I wouldn't know what to do with them. But to thank him I would send him Hummel figurines, you know, those cute little ceramic children, holding umbrellas or petting kittens, or sitting on a swing. And he'd get so angry on the phone, he'd say Mom, don't send me anything you can order from TV. Which upset me, so to express that, I sent him the Hummel sad little clown. And he said that Hummels were originally made by Nazis, and I said they were not, they were made by German nuns who didn't read the newspaper. I just liked the picture of all those Hummels, all lined up in his New York studio apartment, to remind him of where he came from. I'd say Hank, maybe you're still wearing white T-shirts and Levi's, but I remember when you didn't shrink them. I told him, if homosexuality is genetic, then maybe so is home shopping.

And then, well, he got sick. With that terrible disease. And I flew to New York to see him in the hospital, and do you know what I brought? Nothing. I didn't want to embarrass him, in front of his friends. Who were all so sweet, I mean, they all sort of sounded alike and they all kept kissing and hugging me and saying, Henry, we love your Mom, she's a hoot. A hoot. That means I wear polyester without irony. But they were all really very nice, and so good to Hank, and when we were finally alone he looked up at me and said, so what did you bring me? A potholder, a picture frame decorated with twine and plastic daisies, two little bunnies on a sled? And I said no, I know all of that just upsets you, makes you feel like a hick. And he leaned back onto the pillow and he said, oh. It's okay. I just wanted to see you.

And I stayed there until, well, let's use one of those euphemisms, until he passed on. Maybe that's why euphemisms get invented, not because people are ashamed, but because — they hate the real word too much. And I hated that word, and I hated that disease, and for the longest time I just went to work and came home and I didn't touch a thing. Not a needle, not a bobbin, not a hole punch or a pair of pinking shears. I would not bring color or beauty or rickrack into this world. I was just too sad.

And then one day I saw on the television, that quilt. All spread out in Washington, right on the ground in front of the Capitol. Over seventy-two thousand squares, each for a different man, woman, or child. And I looked at it and I thought, my Lord, it's like a cemetery created by the *Ladies Home Journal*. And I took all the fancy trims and laces and bugle beads that Hank had sent me, and I went over to Newberry's and I got a rectangle of hot pink felt. And I made his name in embroidered script, and I stitched on one of his report cards and his mittens and one of his T-shirts which said, "No One Knows I'm Gay." Only I changed it so it said, "No One Knows I'm From Decatur." And in the corner I attached one of those labels I always use, that says, "Especially Handmade Just For You By Barbara Ellen Diggs." And I folded up the whole thing and sent it away, so Lord knows where it is now.

But that was ages ago, and now they have all that new medicine, so people, well, at least some people, can keep going. And we've got whole new ways to hurt people, like that 9/11. And I have to tell you something, and you're going to think I'm awful, but when I first heard about it, on TV, and they said Muslim terrorists had attacked those buildings? I swear to God, I thought they said muslin. Muslin terrorists. And I didn't understand and I thought, they're just using cheap cotton? But of course then I found out what it really was, and I saw that all of those people had died and I wondered, will there be a quilt? And I thought, well, probably not in New York, where everyone is so fancy, I thought, maybe they'll make a duvet. I'm sorry.

And about a year or so later, I went back to New York, because I was a finalist, in a cake-decorating competition. It was cutthroat. The woman next to me, from Ohio, she was so sure that she was going to win, because she'd baked a five-layer devil's food supreme, frosted with the entire Battle of Gettysburg. She'd used mocha pudding and shredded coconut for the battlefield, and the Union forces were Necco wafers, and the Confederates were all Gummi Bears. But the judges said it was contrived. No comment.

And I thought that maybe I had a shot, for my special Easter Sunday extravaganza. I had frosted a lemon meringue sheet cake with an exact replica of Leonardo DaVinci's "The Last Supper," only instead of the apostles everyone at the table was either a chocolate bunny or a marshmallow peep. But then that Gettysburg woman made a stink, and said that my work was sacrilegious, because I'd included Mary Magdalene, but I said, I know that it's controversial, but she's a peanut M&M!

So I lost, and the city reminded me of Hank, and people said that you could sometimes still smell the, what was it, the jet fuel from that day. And I just couldn't go downtown because it was so terrible, and because that's where Hank lived and so I walked over, from the Marriot, to Central Park. And they were having this, I didn't really know what to call it, but people said it was an installation. By this French artist named Christo. And it seems that this Christo person goes all around the world, and he wraps up landmarks in fabric. I'm not kidding. That's what he does, he pays for it and he gets all of these helpers and all of these sewing machines and they wrap up buildings and islands and bridges. I'm not kidding! And I wondered if maybe, when he was younger, for Christmas, if Christo once gave someone a particularly bulky item, like a bicycle or an outdoor barbeque, and he had to wrap it. Eureka! And in the park, he'd put up hundreds of these sort of archways, these aluminum gates, and from each one, from the top, there was a bright orange curtain. And I thought, well, now I know what an installation is — it's just a giant French crafts project.

And I stood there and the sun came out and the breeze was blowing all of those orange curtains and it didn't make any sense, but it was very pretty. Like a county fair, at a graduate school. And then I saw this car, this limousine, driving slowly through the park, and this woman next to me, she said that the man in the car was Christo, with his wife, Jean-Claude. And that they drove through all the time, to watch people's reactions. And as the car got closer the window rolled down and inside I could see this little man, Christo, and I waved. And he waved back, and I didn't know what to say, so I just pointed to all of the gates and I said, "Wow! Yardage!" And the car drove past and I asked the woman, I said, does this installation, and all of this orange fabric, does it make people feel better? And I could tell that she was a New Yorker because she said, *(She uses a tougher New York voice.)* "Yes, it does. Because it's free and they're gonna take it down." And I hadn't really talked about him in so long, especially not to a stranger, but I stood under one of those gates and I told her about Hank. And I asked her if she was there, if she was in the city on 9/11. And she said yes. And I asked, did you lose anyone, and she said yes. That her brother was a firefighter.

And it's strange, but when I got back to Decatur, I started to feel a little cheerier, for the first time in years. My friend Susan Deckerman says that maybe I found closure, and I said, Susan, Oprah is just a person. But I've started to make these sock monkeys *(She picks up a pair of sock monkeys from the table.)* and I take them to our local hospital and I hang them on the patient's IV stands. Because maybe when a sick person sees a sock monkey, they'll smile, and I bet they wouldn't do that if they looked up and saw "Guernica."

And that woman I met in New York, in the park, her name is Eileen and we've kept in touch. And after they took those gates down, Eileen got some of the fabric and sent it to me. And so I made this … *(She holds up a bright orange, quilted oven mitt.)* It's a quilted oven mitt. And I'm gonna send it to Eileen, with a note that says, "You see? That Christo can make something useful." I don't know if I believe in God anymore. But I do believe in cute. I believe in glue. I believe in hot pink felt. And maybe if I was a New Yorker, I would believe in orange shower curtains hanging in Central Park. Amen. *(Curtain.)*

End of Play

THE NEW CENTURY

PLACE

The maternity ward of a Manhattan hospital. There's some sense of walls, maybe with nursery themed wall paper. The newborns are where the audience is.

TIME

Afternoon.

THE NEW CENTURY

Helene Nadler sits or reclines on a bench, upstage, surrounded by shopping bags.

Mr. Charles enters, cautiously. He's incognito, wearing a drab trenchcoat and a hat. He glances around. Thinking that he's alone, he removes his coat and hat, revealing his customary, flamboyant splendor. He sees the babies, and he's delighted. Facing the audience, he speaks to the babies.

MR. CHARLES. Hello … hello there … hello … hello, you … you little sweetheart … you tiny darling … oh you … and you … hello!
HELENE. It's you.
MR. CHARLES. Pardon?
HELENE. I know you.
MR. CHARLES. What?
HELENE. When I was down in Florida, I couldn't sleep. It must've been 3 A.M. and I turned on the TV, and there you were, Mr. Chester …
MR. CHARLES. *(Shielding his face.)* No, I'm sorry, you're wrong. That wasn't me.
HELENE. Excuse me?
MR. CHARLES. You're thinking of someone else, happens all the time, it's a mistaken identity …
HELENE. Mr. Charles!
MR. CHARLES. Oh no no no no no …
HELENE. It is you!
MR. CHARLES. *(Grandly.)* How did you recognize me?
HELENE. You're very distinctive.
MR. CHARLES. And a desperado. You see, I was banned from New York.
HELENE. You were banned? Why?

MR. CHARLES. Do you remember the name of my show?

HELENE. "Too Gay"?

MR. CHARLES. SHHHHH!!!

HELENE. So why did you come back?

MR. CHARLES. It's New York. I couldn't stay away. So I escaped from Palm Beach. It wasn't easy. I traveled by night, sometimes I even wore men's clothing. South Carolina, North Carolina, Virginia — have you seen those people? Until finally, I came here, to this maternity ward, to see the babies. *(Mr. Charles zaps a few babies.)* Ssst … Ssst …

HELENE. What are you doing?

MR. CHARLES. Nothing. I'm sorry.

HELENE. No, no, I'm sorry, I'm … in a terrible state, and I shouldn't be, I have no right. Because last night, my beautiful daughter Leslie and her partner, they gave birth, to that gorgeous baby right over there, in that bassinet … *(She reads the nametag.)* "Rebecca Michael Miracle Cilantro Kinkasha O'Malley-Nadler." Isn't that original? It sounds like an appetizer. No no, I think it's wonderful, I think the two Mommies, they're wonderful, truly, it's just, oh, I'm sorry, I'm babbling …

MR. CHARLES. Tell me.

HELENE. I can't, it's too shameful, it's too selfish, I'm just feeling sorry for myself, and that is disgusting — what, just because I'm a woman and you're a gay man, I'm just supposed to automatically confide in you? Is that how it works? Forget it. Okay. It's just — an hour ago, I was up in that hospital room and all of my kids, they all left, with their friends and their partners, and my husband, he went off to play golf, which believe me I'm fine with, and then Leslie turned to me, and she said "Ma, go home." And I said, No, I can help, I can get you things, and she said, "No, thank you, it's okay, Marsha's here. Go home."

MR. CHARLES. Oh no …

HELENE. Go home? To what? To who? Rhetorical. To a photo album filled with ancient history, with pictures of Leslie learning to hold a tennis racquet, and Veronica when she had a penis, and David in diapers — it's from last year. It's just I thought that, maybe if I came up here, and I saw all of this new life, that maybe it would cheer me up. But it's not working. I look at all of this hope, all of this possibility, and I just want — to tell them. I just want to scream, to every last one of these babies, maybe you were only born

four hours ago, but think very carefully, don't make any mistakes, don't blow it, *(Reading a name.)* — Tiffany Sierra — because your whole life, it's the blink of an eye, and it's all gonna be over so soon ... *(We hear all the babies start to wail; it's quite a cacophony.)*
MR. CHARLES. *(To the babies.)* Happy Birthday! *(Barbara Ellen Diggs enters, in a wheelchair upstage.)*
BARBARA ELLEN. Don't mind me.
HELENE. *(Regarding Barbara Ellen, to Mr. Charles.)* Jesus. And look at her. In a wheelchair.
MR. CHARLES. Can you imagine?
HELENE. I would kill myself.
HELENE and MR. CHARLES. *(Both suddenly very cheerful, to Barbara Ellen.)* Hi!
BARBARA ELLEN. Oh, hello!
MR. CHARLES. Can we help you?
HELENE. Can I push you? I always say that to my children.
BARBARA ELLEN. Oh, thank you, that's so sweet, but no, thank you, both of you, I'm fine, I'm just fine.
MR. CHARLES. *(To Barbara Ellen.)* And you're perky.
BARBARA ELLEN. No, I'm not.
MR. CHARLES. Excuse me?
BARBARA ELLEN. I'm sorry, what am I saying, I'm a spunky, good-natured person, I just meant that — if I could just keep busy — excuse me, either of you, do you have any yarn? No, I'm fine, look at all of these babies! Couldn't you just eat them right up?
HELENE. *(To Barbara Ellen.)* Are you all right? Would you like a snack?
MR. CHARLES. Some water? *(Helene and Mr. Charles move to their bags and belongings to find snacks and bottled water.)*
BARBARA ELLEN. Oh, no — sure. It's just I got into town last night, and this morning, I went to Madison Square Garden, for the big annual Cat Show.
HELENE. *(Handing her a bag of nuts.)* Here you go.
BARBARA ELLEN. Thank you. Do you have anything sweet?
HELENE. Sure. *(To Mr. Charles, whispering.)* She's in a wheelchair.
BARBARA ELLEN. I was competing in a kitty couture fashion show, because I've started making little outfits for my cats.
HELENE. *(In disbelief.)* You make outfits for your — no, I'm sorry. Who am I to judge?
BARBARA ELLEN. Are you Jewish?

HELENE. I resent your assumption. Just because someone is critical and articulate and always hungry — fine, I'm Jewish.

MR. CHARLES. And your show?

BARBARA ELLEN. Well, by the final round, it had all come down to me and this one other kitty couturier, this math teacher from Maryland, whose specialty was kitty swimwear. And I'm sorry, but I just said it right out loud, I said a cat does not need a two piece bathing suit. And he said, well, so why does your cat need a pink satin strapless gown, and I said, for evening. And then just as she hit the runway, my cat, my beautiful little Abyssinian, she just got so nervous that she bolted, right out of the exhibition hall, down the escalator and out into the street. And I ran after her, and just as I grabbed her, I got sideswiped by a taxicab.

HELENE. Oh no!

BARBARA ELLEN. But all sorts of people rushed right over to help me, all of these wonderful New Yorkers, you know, it really is a melting pot, because every one of them smelled different. And then an ambulance came and brought me here, and all of the doctors and the nurses have been so helpful.

HELENE. And how's your cat?

BARBARA ELLEN. Oh she's just fine, thank God. She's resting.

MR. CHARLES. And her evening gown?

BARBARA ELLEN. I don't want to talk about it.

MR. CHARLES. Give it time.

BARBARA ELLEN. And nothing's broken, I just have a bruised hip, it's just … oh, I'm being such a baby.

HELENE. No you're not, not at all …

MR. CHARLES. You've had a dreadful day …

BARBARA ELLEN. It's just, well, when you're in a hospital, everything is so upsetting. For the sick people, and the families, except for the maternity ward. It's the only floor where everyone's happy to be there. And it's just, oh, I shouldn't even say this, it was so long ago …

MR. CHARLES. What?

BARBARA ELLEN. It's just — this is the hospital where my son died.

HELENE. Oh no. I'm so sorry.

MR. CHARLES. You poor dear …

BARBARA ELLEN. He was such a sweet boy. I mean, he was special. Different.

MR. CHARLES. Different?

BARBARA ELLEN. *(To Mr. Charles.)* Are you gay?

MR. CHARLES. Oh no. I'm with Cirque de Soleil.

BARBARA ELLEN. I'm sorry …

MR. CHARLES. No, of course I'm gay. Very gay. Too gay.

BARBARA ELLEN. I like your hair.

MR. CHARLES. You do?

BARBARA ELLEN. Did you make it?

MR. CHARLES. *(Touching his hairpiece.)* Yes. It's Abyssinian.

BARBARA ELLEN. *(Charmed by him.)* You're terrible!

MR. CHARLES. Yes I am.

BARBARA ELLEN. You sound just like my son.

HELENE. He does?

BARBARA ELLEN. *(To Helene.)* Do you have children?

HELENE. One lesbian daughter, one transsexual lesbian son, and another gay son who's into bondage and poop.

BARBARA ELLEN. Oh my Lord. So what do they give you for Mother's Day?

HELENE. Cash.

MR. CHARLES. Look at us. All of us.

HELENE. Look at our lives.

BARBARA ELLEN. What do we do with this world? What do we tell all of these babies? You're born …

HELENE. You go shopping …

MR. CHARLES. You have tea …

BARBARA ELLEN. You create a wedding gown for your cat with a catnip bouquet and a three-foot ivory silk train …

HELENE. *(After a beat.)* Your cat got married?

BARBARA ELLEN. To our labradoodle. Who wore tails, a bowtie and a top hat.

HELENE. *(Another beat.)* Who married them?

BARBARA ELLEN. Our parakeet. Episcopal.

MR. CHARLES. It won't last.

BARBARA ELLEN. Do you think that, on any level, that these babies can understand us?

HELENE. Well, my mother said that babies have all the knowledge in the world. Except that right before they're born, God smacks them and they forget everything.

BARBARA ELLEN. Did she really believe that?

HELENE. She'd tell me, "Helene, God must've smacked you really hard."

BARBARA ELLEN. Well, if we could get through — what would you tell them? What advice would you give?

HELENE. Don't get old.

BARBARA ELLEN. Don't love anyone.

MR. CHARLES. And if you have no morals but you'd still like to run for public office, move to Florida. *(Shane enters, wearing all sorts of outlandishly gaudy new clothes and carrying shopping bags. He's wildly excited, like a kid.)*

SHANE. Yo, Chuck!

MR. CHARLES. Shane?

HELENE. You're that boy, from his TV show. You were dressed like a gladiator.

SHANE. *(Indicating Mr. Charles.)* He made me do that …

HELENE. You looked very handsome …

MR. CHARLES. *(To Shane.)* You see?

SHANE. I never been to New York before! Hi, I'm Shane …

HELENE. Helene.

BARBARA ELLEN. Barbara Ellen.

SHANE. Whoa. Man, are you like in a wheelchair?

BARBARA ELLEN. Well, at the moment …

SHANE. Sweet! So I like come up here with Chuck, and I've been goin' like all over the place! All the like, landmarks! *(He shows everyone his postcards.)* Like Times Square, and the Empire State Building, *(To Barbara Ellen.)* look, it's got a ramp. And then I saw all these trucks, and there was this dead hooker, with her neck all broken, lyin' on the ground in a pool of her own blood.

HELEN. They were shooting *Law and Order.*

SHANE. It was so cool! But then I go, yo, I'm in New York, I gotta do it, I gotta see it, so I go down — to Ground Zero.

HELENE. Oh my.

SHANE. And at first I'm confused, 'cause I get outta the subway and I'm like, where is it? And then I go, right, that's the whole deal, there's nothin' there. It's gone. And it's like I'm tryin' to look at — what used to be there.

BARBARA ELLEN. Yes.

SHANE. And then, I look up. And I swear to God, I see it. Right there.

HELENE. What?

MR. CHARLES. Shane, what do you see?

SHANE. At first I can't believe it, I go, what is that, but it's just

44

shining, just glowing, right over the whole damn thing, over alla that construction shit, there was this bigass neon sign, and it said — "Century 21."

BARBARA ELLEN. Century 21?

SHANE. And I'm goin', what, but I walk over, and I go inside, and it's like the coolest store I've ever seen, in like my whole entire life! They got everything, like Versace and Dolce and Nike and sweats and shades and — alla this! Like everything I'm wearin'! For like, twenty-five bucks! *Total!*

HELENE. And so this discount store, it made you feel better? About — life?

SHANE. I don't know. At first I'm goin', this don't make sense, what happened out there, and what's goin' on in here, and people posin' for pictures in front of the pit, like it's Epcot, and I'm like, I don't know what's goin' on. And I go, maybe we should all just sorta stop. And be respectful. And I try, I swear I did, I'm standin' in that store, with my eyes closed, sorta like prayin'. But then there's all this music, on the sound system, and I open my eyes and it's like — there's this big fat lady, from like I don't know, Czechoslovakia, or the Dominican Republic, and she's got like six kids, and she's tryin' on this dress, and it's got flowers all over, and she's totally packed into it. And you can tell that she's gonna wear it to like, a party or a weddin', and her kids are all goin' like, Mami, lookin' good, and she's laughin', 'cause her kids are right, 'cause she looks so good. And I'm goin', is she bein' disrespectful, or is she — lookin' good!

HELENE. I don't know …

SHANE. Okay, like what's your biggest problem? Like right this second?

HELENE. Aside from, say, world peace and disease and hunger? I'm old.

SHANE. Not at Century 21. You could get like a smokin' new outfit, with all like the accessories and the shoes and a bag.

HELENE. Excuse me, are you actually saying that if I just got all decked out, in some designer outfit, that I'd feel better? And that somehow my new shoes would make the world a better place?

SHANE. Yeah!

HELENE. That is ridiculous. And insane. And offensive.

SHANE. It is?

HELENE. Because that is not an answer. That's an evasion. That's denial. And I'm sorry to be such a drag, and maybe I'm just letting my own personal agita color everything, but — I just can't pretend. Not anymore. Buildings fall. People die. Life ends. And a pretty new handbag isn't going to solve my problems or your problems or anyone else's!

SHANE. I'm sorry …

MR. CHARLES. Shane, perhaps we should go …

BARBARA ELLEN. But it was so nice to meet you … *(As Mr. Charles and Shane are almost gone:)*

HELENE. Wait.

SHANE. Yeah?

HELENE. So do they really have bags?

SHANE. They got like this Ralph Lauren bag, from this year, it was like twenty-six hundred bucks, if you could find it, but at Century 21 — eighty-nine dollars and fifty cents.

HELENE. It is not.

SHANE. Is!

HELENE. And it's not a knock-off, or one of those bags with the cheap top-stitching which they just make for the outlet stores in Connecticut, it's not just some crappy mall bag?

SHANE. Hey, in my like, occupation, I been in some nice houses, and I know real Ralph.

HELENE. I love real Ralph. I worship real Ralph. Ralph Lauren is a Jewish superhero. Ralph Lauren is a Jewish saint.

BARBARA ELLEN. Wait.

HELENE. What?

BARBARA ELLEN. Ralph Lauren is Jewish?

HELENE. Ralph Lauren could make a yarmulke for your cat.

SHANE. And Chuck, you know how you been actin' all like, nobody wants to be gay anymore, not like your kinda gay?

MR. CHARLES. They don't. No one does.

SHANE. Not at Century 21! I saw these guys, they're tryin' on tank tops and cashmere and cologne — it's like, all the nice, normal gay guys and even some of the straight dudes, they sneak down there, to get a fix. You could hear 'em, in the dressin' rooms, they couldn't control themselves …

MR. CHARLES. Did they do nelly breaks?

SHANE. It's like if Patti LuPone was a *store.*

MR. CHARLES. Oh my!

SHANE. *(To Barbara Ellen.)* And you, I bet if you could like, talk to God, or Allah or whoever, I bet you'd be all like, can I have some legs, please, right?

BARBARA ELLEN. But …

SHANE. Could I like maybe get up outta this chair? Like probably just the way it happens when you're dreamin'. Man, that's a tough one. I don't know about that. I'm like, really, really, really sorry. *(Shane turns away, upset.)*

BARBARA ELLEN. Your scarf — is that tie-dye? *(Barbara Ellen stands up, and reaches for Shane's colorful scarf.)* That looks handmade. *(Shane is staring at Barbara Ellen, staggered and awestruck by the miracle of her standing up and walking.)*

SHANE. Shit. Shit. Oh my fuckin' *shit!*

MR. CHARLES. Shane?

SHANE. Century 21 is fuckin' *awesome! (For the first time, he spots the babies.)* Whoa! Babies!

BARBARA ELLEN. *(Holding Shane's scarf.)* Could I have this? Oh no, I'm sorry, I have no right, you take this right back …

SHANE. No, no man, you gotta keep it.

BARBARA ELLEN. Oh, you are just as cute as a bug, and you're almost exactly the same age, as my son. When he — left.

SHANE. You mean like, when he kicked?

BARBARA ELLEN. Yes.

SHANE. Did you love him?

BARBARA ELLEN. Yes.

SHANE. Was he gay?

BARBARA ELLEN. Yes.

SHANE. Was he hot?

BARBARA ELLEN. Yes.

SHANE. Then it's okay.

BARBARA ELLEN. It is?

SHANE. 'Cause see, some people think that heaven is all like white and fluffy, but I think that sounds kinda boring. So I figure maybe it's more like, I don't know, a club, so there's hot music, and God is kinda like Chuck.

BARBARA ELLEN. I like that.

MR. CHARLES. Shane, you're embarrassing me. I'm not God. I mean, look at the world. God obviously has no taste.

HELENE. *(To Shane, pointing to a baby.)* That's my grandchild. Isn't she gorgeous?

SHANE. Yeah. So are you gonna like, babysit for free and tell all

your friends where she's gonna go to college and stuff?
HELENE. No! Of course I am. And maybe I can tell her — about my life, and everything I've been through. And everything we've all been through. I'll just bum her right out. Yeah, she's gonna love visiting Grandma. But maybe I should have a little faith. Because my grandchild, and all of these children — they are Century 21.
SHANE. But the Chanel sunglasses? The big round white ones? Buy 'em on the street. Even cheaper.
HELENE. You're a very smart boy. You should have your own show.
MR. CHARLES. I keep telling him.
SHANE. Maybe it's time. And maybe I could have like, special guest stars! 'Cause guess what I got? *(He grabs CD's from one of his shopping bags.)* From this dude who had 'em all spread out on this like blanket? Hot new CD's!
MR. CHARLES. And you can be dressed as the Greek god Apollo!
SHANE. *(Upset.)* Man …
HELENE. *(Reassuring Shane.)* That would be very hot …
BARBARA ELLEN. Spray glue and body glitter. I have a catalogue.
SHANE. *(Now getting excited about the idea.)* Really? And as one of my Special Guest Stars — Barbara Ellen, the miracle lady of Century 21!
BARBARA ELLEN. Well, I already have my own interactive website.
SHANE. What's it called?
BARBARA ELLEN. "Gluetube."
SHANE. And Helene — the smokin' hot Jewish lady!
HELENE. Me? On TV? When I lose five pounds.
SHANE. And you asked for it, the gayest gay guy in the whole entire universe …
MR. CHARLES. And the last …
SHANE. Mr. Chuck! *(Joann enters, pushing her baby in a stroller. A fabric hood conceals the baby.)*
JOANN. *(Stunned at seeing Mr. Charles and Shane.)* Oh my god …
MR. CHARLES. *(Equally shocked.)* Hello?
HELENE. Yes?
SHANE. Hey! You're her! You're that girl! From Florida! You used to work at the TV station.
JOANN. I left. I was living with my Mom and trying to work and raise my baby and we were all going crazy. *(To Helene and Barbara Ellen.)* Hi!
BARBARA ELLEN and HELENE. Hi.

JOANN. So you know how, when they're really in trouble, some people ask, what would Jesus do? *(Helene gestures to Barbara Ellen.)*
BARBARA ELLEN. Oh, uh huh …
JOANN. Well, I asked myself, what would Mr. Charles do?
MR. CHARLES. You did?
HELENE. Oh my …
JOANN. And so — I moved to New York. And it was all so new and scary, and I don't have any money, so I'm really living in New Jersey. But I come into the city every chance I get, just to look at it.
MR. CHARLES. But what are you doing in the maternity ward?
JOANN. I want my baby to be a New Yorker, so I bring him here to the clinic. Because I want him to meet all sorts of different people. *(To Barbara Ellen.)* Like, where are you from?
BARBARA ELLEN. Decatur, Illinois. We're the Soybean Capitol.
JOANN. *(To Helene.)* And what about you?
HELENE. I'm from Massapequa, Long Island.
JOANN. *(Thrilled.)* "Massapequa." That sounds like a wonderful old Indian name. But what does it mean in English?
HELENE. "Don't touch my hair."
JOANN. You see? That's New York. All of you. And that's what I want for my baby.
MR. CHARLES. And how is your baby?
JOANN. Oh, he's wonderful. Look. *(She pulls the fabric hood off the stroller, revealing the baby, who's now wearing very brightly colored clothes, including huge rhinestone sunglasses, a vivid scarf and a hint of rouge, along with a tiny hairpiece, so he looks just like Mr. Charles. The effect is uncanny.)*
HELENE. Oh my God …
BARBARA ELLEN. He looks like a birthday cake. Or a Christmas sweater.
MR. CHARLES. He looks like me.
SHANE. Whoa. *Whoa. (To Mr. Charles.)* Chuck. You did it. It *worked.*
JOANN. He's in color!
HELENE. *(To Joann.)* This is your child? You're the mother?
JOANN. Yes.
HELENE. *(Putting her arm around Joann.)* God, we have so much to talk about.
MR. CHARLES. Shane? Ladies? Mr. Max? Maestro? *(The lights go to black. From the darkness, a suspenseful musical vamp begins, and*

49

we hear:)

ANNOUNCER. And now, ladies and gentlemen, it's four in the morning, you can't sleep, so turn to cable channel 47! Because you wanted it, you begged for it, by overwhelming popular demand, it's time for the hottest new public access program in all of South Florida, it's time for The Shane Show! Starring everybody's favorite South Florida male superstar, Shane! *(A spotlight come up on Shane, dancing. A sign behind him reads "THE SHANE SHOW!" Hot dance music blasts.)* With Shane's special guest stars, including the former receptionist and the mother of Mr. Max — Joann! *(Joann appears, dancing with Max.)* She's heaven, she's happening — hold on to your handbags, because here's Helene! *(Helene appears and dances. She holds up her gorgeous new Ralph Lauren bag.)* She's clever, she's crafty, she can't stop creating — straight from Decatur, she's Barbara Ellen! *(Barbara Ellen appears and dances. She's now wearing a hand-crocheted poncho, or a particularly festive Christmas sweater.)* He's too gay, he's too much, and he's all yours — it's Mr. Charles! *(Mr. Charles appears, dancing.)*

MR. CHARLES. Wait! *(The music pauses.)* We're all so proud to be here, as guests on this Palm Beach premiere. And I would just like to take this opportunity to thank our star and our host …

BARBARA ELLEN. The hottest thing in South Florida …

HELENE. And a very bright young man, who will soon be attending Palm Beach community college …

SHANE. *(This is news to him.)* What?

HELENE. Just a thought.

ALL. *Here's Shane!*

SHANE. *(Very choked up.)* Thank you, thank all of you for bein' here on my very first show, and thank all of you out there, for watchin'. 'Cause we're all in this together, and there's only one way to fix this whole damn planet. And it goes something like this … *(The music roars back on, and Shane executes a dance move. His guests all join in, doing the same move. Everyone's dancing joyously. Curtain.)*

End of Play

PROPERTY LIST

MR. CHARLES, CURRENTLY OF PALM BEACH
Letter
Telegram
Stack of letters
Video camera
Silver tea set on tray
Cup and saucer
Lemon wedge
Bouquet of roses
Newspaper
Car keys
Baby

CRAFTY
Board holding 3 doorknobs with crocheted covers
Large quilted microwave bonnet
Crocheted cover for roll of toilet paper
Toaster with hand-crocheted black and white cover with bowtie
Sweatshirt with snowman and Santa appliqué
Scrapbook with pictures
2 sock monkeys
Bright orange quilted oven mitt

THE NEW CENTURY
Snacks
Bag of nuts
Bottle of water
Shopping bags
Colorful scarf
CDs
Baby stroller with fabric hood

SOUND EFFECTS

MR. CHARLES, CURRENTLY OF PALM BEACH
A cacophony of babies wailing
Big band theme music
Hot dance music
Military music
Cheery music
Oscar Night music

THE NEW CENTURY
Suspenseful musical vamp
Hot dance music

NEW PLAYS

★ **GUARDIANS by Peter Morris.** In this unflinching look at war, a disgraced American soldier discloses the truth about Abu Ghraib prison, and a clever English journalist reveals how he faked a similar story for the London tabloids. "Compelling, sympathetic and powerful." –*NY Times.* "Sends you into a state of moral turbulence." –*Sunday Times (UK).* "Nothing short of remarkable." –*Village Voice.* [1M, 1W] ISBN: 978-0-8222-2177-7

★ **BLUE DOOR by Tanya Barfield.** Three generations of men (all played by one actor), from slavery through Black Power, challenge Lewis, a tenured professor of mathematics, to embark on a journey combining past and present. "A teasing flare for words." –*Village Voice.* "Unfailingly thought-provoking." –*LA Times.* "The play moves with the speed and logic of a dream." –*Seattle Weekly.* [2M] ISBN: 978-0-8222-2209-5

★ **THE INTELLIGENT DESIGN OF JENNY CHOW by Rolin Jones.** This irreverent "techno-comedy" chronicles one brilliant woman's quest to determine her heritage and face her fears with the help of her astounding creation called Jenny Chow. "Boldly imagined." –*NY Times.* "Fantastical and funny." –*Variety.* "Harvests many laughs and finally a few tears." –*LA Times.* [3M, 3W] ISBN: 978-0-8222-2071-8

★ **SOUVENIR by Stephen Temperley.** Florence Foster Jenkins, a wealthy society eccentric, suffers under the delusion that she is a great coloratura soprano—when in fact the opposite is true. "Hilarious and deeply touching. Incredibly moving and breathtaking." –*NY Daily News.* "A sweet love letter of a play." –*NY Times.* "Wildly funny. Completely charming." –*Star-Ledger.* [1M, 1W] ISBN: 978-0-8222-2157-9

★ **ICE GLEN by Joan Ackermann.** In this touching period comedy, a beautiful poetess dwells in idyllic obscurity on a Berkshire estate with a band of unlikely cohorts. "A beautifully written story of nature and change." –*Talkin' Broadway.* "A lovely play which will leave you with a lot to think about." –*CurtainUp.* "Funny, moving and witty." –*Metroland (Boston).* [4M, 3W] ISBN: 978-0-8222-2175-3

★ **THE LAST DAYS OF JUDAS ISCARIOT by Stephen Adly Guirgis.** Set in a time-bending, darkly comic world between heaven and hell, this play reexamines the plight and fate of the New Testament's most infamous sinner. "An unforced eloquence that finds the poetry in lowdown street talk." –*NY Times.* "A real jaw-dropper." –*Variety.* "An extraordinary play." –*Guardian (UK).* [10M, 5W] ISBN: 978-0-8222-2082-4

DRAMATISTS PLAY SERVICE, INC.
440 Park Avenue South, New York, NY 10016 212-683-8960 Fax 212-213-1539
postmaster@dramatists.com www.dramatists.com

NEW PLAYS

★ **THE GREAT AMERICAN TRAILER PARK MUSICAL music and lyrics by David Nehls, book by Betsy Kelso.** Pippi, a stripper on the run, has just moved into Armadillo Acres, wreaking havoc among the tenants of Florida's most exclusive trailer park. "Adultery, strippers, murderous ex-boyfriends, Costco and the Ice Capades. Undeniable fun." –*NY Post.* "Joyful and unashamedly vulgar." –*The New Yorker.* "Sparkles with treasure." –*New York Sun.* [2M, 5W] ISBN: 978-0-8222-2137-1

★ **MATCH by Stephen Belber.** When a young Seattle couple meet a prominent New York choreographer, they are led on a fraught journey that will change their lives forever. "Uproariously funny, deeply moving, enthralling theatre." –*NY Daily News.* "Prolific laughs and ear-to-ear smiles." –*NY Magazine.* [2M, 1W] ISBN: 978-0-8222-2020-6

★ **MR. MARMALADE by Noah Haidle.** Four-year-old Lucy's imaginary friend, Mr. Marmalade, doesn't have much time for her—not to mention he has a cocaine addiction and a penchant for pornography. "Alternately hilarious and heartbreaking." –*The New Yorker.* "A mature and accomplished play." –*LA Times.* "Scathingly observant comedy." –*Miami Herald.* [4M, 2W] ISBN: 978-0-8222-2142-5

★ **MOONLIGHT AND MAGNOLIAS by Ron Hutchinson.** Three men cloister themselves as they work tirelessly to reshape a screenplay that's just not working—*Gone with the Wind.* "Consumers of vintage Hollywood insider stories will eat up Hutchinson's diverting conjecture." –*Variety.* "A lot of fun." –*NY Post.* "A Hollywood dream-factory farce." –*Chicago Sun-Times.* [3M, 1W] ISBN: 978-0-8222-2084-8

★ **THE LEARNED LADIES OF PARK AVENUE by David Grimm, translated and freely adapted from Molière's Les Femmes Savantes.** Dicky wants to marry Betty, but her mother's plan is for Betty to wed a most pompous man. "A brave, brainy and barmy revision." –*Hartford Courant.* "A rare but welcome bird in contemporary theatre." –*New Haven Register.* "Roll over Cole Porter." –*Boston Globe.* [5M, 5W] ISBN: 978-0-8222-2135-7

★ **REGRETS ONLY by Paul Rudnick.** A sparkling comedy of Manhattan manners that explores the latest topics in marriage, friendships and squandered riches. "One of the funniest quip-meisters on the planet." –*NY Times.* "Precious moments of hilarity. Devastatingly accurate political and social satire." –*BackStage.* "Great fun." –*CurtainUp.* [3M, 3W] ISBN: 978-0-8222-2223-1

DRAMATISTS PLAY SERVICE, INC.
440 Park Avenue South, New York, NY 10016 212-683-8960 Fax 212-213-1539
postmaster@dramatists.com www.dramatists.com

NEW PLAYS

★ **AFTER ASHLEY by Gina Gionfriddo.** A teenager is unwillingly thrust into the national spotlight when a family tragedy becomes talk-show fodder. "A work that virtually any audience would find accessible." –*NY Times.* "Deft characterization and caustic humor." –*NY Sun.* "A smart satirical drama." –*Variety.* [4M, 2W] ISBN: 978-0-8222-2099-2

★ **THE RUBY SUNRISE by Rinne Groff.** Twenty-five years after Ruby struggles to realize her dream of inventing the first television, her daughter faces similar battles of faith as she works to get Ruby's story told on network TV. "Measured and intelligent, optimistic yet clear-eyed." –*NY Magazine.* "Maintains an exciting sense of ingenuity." –*Village Voice.* "Sinuous theatrical flair." –*Broadway.com.* [3M, 4W] ISBN: 978-0-8222-2140-1

★ **MY NAME IS RACHEL CORRIE taken from the writings of Rachel Corrie, edited by Alan Rickman and Katharine Viner.** This solo piece tells the story of Rachel Corrie who was killed in Gaza by an Israeli bulldozer set to demolish a Palestinian home. "Heartbreaking urgency. An invigoratingly detailed portrait of a passionate idealist." –*NY Times.* "Deeply authentically human." –*USA Today.* "A stunning dramatization." –*CurtainUp.* [1W] ISBN: 978-0-8222-2222-4

★ **ALMOST, MAINE by John Cariani.** This charming midwinter night's dream of a play turns romantic clichés on their ear as it chronicles the painfully hilarious amorous adventures (and misadventures) of residents of a remote northern town that doesn't quite exist. "A whimsical approach to the joys and perils of romance." –*NY Times.* "Sweet, poignant and witty." –*NY Daily News.* "Aims for the heart by way of the funny bone." –*Star-Ledger.* [2M, 2W] ISBN: 978-0-8222-2156-2

★ **Mitch Albom's TUESDAYS WITH MORRIE by Jeffrey Hatcher and Mitch Albom, based on the book by Mitch Albom.** The true story of Brandeis University professor Morrie Schwartz and his relationship with his student Mitch Albom. "A touching, life-affirming, deeply emotional drama." –*NY Daily News.* "You'll laugh. You'll cry." –*Variety.* "Moving and powerful." –*NY Post.* [2M] ISBN: 978-0-8222-2188-3

★ **DOG SEES GOD: CONFESSIONS OF A TEENAGE BLOCKHEAD by Bert V. Royal.** An abused pianist and a pyromaniac ex-girlfriend contribute to the teen-angst of America's most hapless kid. "A welcome antidote to the notion that the *Peanuts* gang provides merely American cuteness." –*NY Times.* "Hysterically funny." –*NY Post.* "The *Peanuts* kids have finally come out of their shells." –*Time Out.* [4M, 4W] ISBN: 978-0-8222-2152-4

DRAMATISTS PLAY SERVICE, INC.
440 Park Avenue South, New York, NY 10016 212-683-8960 Fax 212-213-1539
postmaster@dramatists.com www.dramatists.com

NEW PLAYS

★ **RABBIT HOLE by David Lindsay-Abaire.** Winner of the 2007 Pulitzer Prize. Becca and Howie Corbett have everything a couple could want until a life-shattering accident turns their world upside down. "An intensely emotional examination of grief, laced with wit." –*Variety.* "A transcendent and deeply affecting new play." –*Entertainment Weekly.* "Painstakingly beautiful." –*BackStage.* [2M, 3W] ISBN: 978-0-8222-2154-8

★ **DOUBT, A Parable by John Patrick Shanley.** Winner of the 2005 Pulitzer Prize and Tony Award. Sister Aloysius, a Bronx school principal, takes matters into her own hands when she suspects the young Father Flynn of improper relations with one of the male students. "All the elements come invigoratingly together like clockwork." –*Variety.* "Passionate, exquisite, important, engrossing." –*NY Newsday.* [1M, 3W] ISBN: 978-0-8222-2219-4

★ **THE PILLOWMAN by Martin McDonagh.** In an unnamed totalitarian state, an author of horrific children's stories discovers that someone has been making his stories come true. "A blindingly bright black comedy." –*NY Times.* "McDonagh's least forgiving, bravest play." –*Variety.* "Thoroughly startling and genuinely intimidating." –*Chicago Tribune.* [4M, 5 bit parts (2M, 1W, 1 boy, 1 girl)] ISBN: 978-0-8222-2100-5

★ **GREY GARDENS book by Doug Wright, music by Scott Frankel, lyrics by Michael Korie.** The hilarious and heartbreaking story of Big Edie and Little Edie Bouvier Beale, the eccentric aunt and cousin of Jacqueline Kennedy Onassis, once bright names on the social register who became East Hampton's most notorious recluses. "An experience no passionate theatergoer should miss." –*NY Times.* "A unique and unmissable musical." –*Rolling Stone.* [4M, 3W, 2 girls] ISBN: 978-0-8222-2181-4

★ **THE LITTLE DOG LAUGHED by Douglas Carter Beane.** Mitchell Green could make it big as the hot new leading man in Hollywood if Diane, his agent, could just keep him in the closet. "Devastatingly funny." –*NY Times.* "An out-and-out delight." –*NY Daily News.* "Full of wit and wisdom." –*NY Post.* [2M, 2W] ISBN: 978-0-8222-2226-2

★ **SHINING CITY by Conor McPherson.** A guilt-ridden man reaches out to a therapist after seeing the ghost of his recently deceased wife. "Haunting, inspired and glorious." –*NY Times.* "Simply breathtaking and astonishing." –*Time Out.* "A thoughtful, artful, absorbing new drama." –*Star-Ledger.* [3M, 1W] ISBN: 978-0-8222-2187-6

DRAMATISTS PLAY SERVICE, INC.
440 Park Avenue South, New York, NY 10016 212-683-8960 Fax 212-213-1539
postmaster@dramatists.com   www.dramatists.com